we're not real anyways

we're not real anyways

maddie mitchell

A Publication of The Poetry Box®

Poems ©2021 Madeline Mitchell
All rights reserved.

Editing & Book Design: Shawn Aveningo Sanders
Cover Design: Robert R. Sanders (RobertSandersPhoto.com)
Author & Cover Photo: Emily Hedges (ebh-photography.com)

Note: The use of lowercase for headings, titles, and proper nouns throughout the remainder of this book is employed to represent the aesthetic writing style of the poet.

No part of this book may be reproduced in any manner whatsoever without permission from the author, except in the case of brief quotations embodied in critical essays, reviews and articles.

ISBN: 978-1-948461-89-4
Library of Congress Control Number: 2021905259
Printed in the United States of America.
Wholesale Distribution via Ingram.

Published by The Poetry Box®, July 2021
Portland, Oregon
ThePoetryBox.com

to the amazing people who have helped me through this journey and who continue to lead me on the path of recovery,

to those who are struggling or have struggled,

and to the girl who saved me:
"fake it till we make it; we're not real anyways"

contents

note from the author	13
moral of the story	15
adulthood	16
success	17
baby blue beetle	18
an old piano	19
more	20
i fucked up my teens	21
daydream	22
to all the boys who pulled a gun on me	23
song lyrics	24
i am in high school again	25
daily routine	26
bakery	27
soft sky blue	28
thief	29
redemption	30
shower thoughts	31
my skin	32
ignorance	33
i am	34
caffeine addiction	35
greetings	36
prom queen	37

old wishes	38
greetings (pt. 2)	39
beginnings	40
what am i?	41
mantra	42
ww3	43
privacy	44
and no.	45
her?	46
breathe	47
beauty in darkness	48
real	49
daydream (pt. 2)	50
you eat for me	51
i don't want...	52
true beauty	53
scrambled eggs	54
most	55
for her	56
mine	57
querencia	58
existing obsolete	59
idk	60
give up	61
let me be selfish	62
fake	63
clinomania	64

paintings	65
past/future	66
scrambling eggs	67
sad	68
laughing	69
who, what, when, where, why?	70
desire	71
life fucking sucks	72
one day	73
we are enough	74
still	75
concede	76
how?	77
rock bottom	78
daydream (pt. 3)	79
what's different this time?	80
missing you	81
my inspiration	82
growth	83
wind whisperer	84
wishes	85
i'm fine	86
loser	87
existence	88
there is no one answer	89
open my fridge	90
recovery	91

i would buy happiness	92
dear kids	93
stop sign	94
when i was a kid,	95
canvas	96
beautiful music	97
reasons to not die:	98
reasons to live:	99
i could never	100
i flee	101
i knew when...	102
always	103
plead	104
magic eraser	105
raindrop	106
starving	107
search history	108
it exists	109
this is it	110
dear future sad me,	111
give zero fucks	112
she is	113
they raised me	114
fake	115
transparency	116
favorite place?	117
favorite place.	118

meeting myself	119
energetic is	120
hopeful	121
girls	122
she	123
butterflies	124
i love you is	125
hostage	126
together	127
desperation	128
dear 13-year-old,	129
future promises	130
i would live for myself	131
Praise for *we-re not real anyways*	133
about the author	135

note from the author

dear readers,

we're not real anyways discusses a wide array of topics. some of these topics include eating disorders, depression, anxiety, and trauma. if you are currently dealing with, or in recovery from a mental illness please be careful while reading this book. consider discussing with your therapist/support system if you are in the right mindset to read about these topics. additionally, please reach out to a trusted support person if any of the following poems are triggering to you. read with grace and kindness towards yourself.

with love,
maddie

moral of the story

this is the story of a girl who hates herself. she was worth nothing when she was born and somehow, she dug herself further into debt. she knew her only penance was to give— give everything to everyone. she wanted to see the world smile. but she found she was the hindrance.

she tried to disappear, so he could finally be happy.

she wanted to fade away until a girl asked her to stay.

maybe she won't always hate herself.

adulthood

i shouldn't want to throw up my birthday cake. i shouldn't run to the bathroom after eating three bites to examine how much weight i gained. i shouldn't tell myself i can't eat the rest of the week to make up for it. i shouldn't have to endure discussions about how many calories must be in the cake i baked myself. i shouldn't hesitate to bring the fork to my mouth. i shouldn't contemplate how i could throw it away without anyone noticing. i shouldn't want to kill myself for eating.

crying over birthday cake shouldn't be the first thing i do as an adult.

success

when did success become measured by Instagram followers and test scores? the number of days you could go without eating? success is throwing my lunch into the garbage can and passing out in gym class mid-run. success is crying into a bowl of pasta and hanging up on my friends when they ask me to come to dinner. success is dress sizes, leadership roles, trophies—titles. success is exhaustion that gets you admitted to the hospital. success is digestive systems that have gone to shit and IV fluids pumping through translucent veins. success is cuts and burned skin—a rope around my neck.

and failure?

failure is eating a fucking sandwich

baby blue beetle

i'm 16. i buy a car. i learn how to drive.

no.

i'm 16. i buy a car, kinda-sorta. my parents tell me to get a permit. i do, i fail; self-esteem floods down the drain. who fails the permit test? i didn't learn my right from my left, i learned AP multiple choice answers and how to fill out a scantron in time.

i get my permit. i don't drive. two years later i do—well, two years later i am on the interstate. damn, cars go so fast. you don't know what that person is going to do. i have no control. the gas pedal squeaks. we could crash. what if i just drove into that tree? i am not here anyway. what is that taste in my mouth? where am i?

"red light! red light! did you even see it?"

"yes."

an old piano

dust has settled on Beethoven's 9th symphony laying on the crumbling music stand. i sit on the stool, the cushion barely supporting me, i let my hands settle softly on the keys. i have to push them down hard to hear a noise. they are still sticky from that afternoon when i was four. i told you i felt sick and you said i needed to practice. i threw up everywhere. i should have realized then your impossible expectations. i now realize my need to fulfill them. i would kill myself trying to meet them—trying to make you love me.

more

    love,
        cute
            radiance
                natural beauty
                      ageless
                          flawless
                    health
                face, body,
            legs
        perfection
gorgeous?
    new self
    facelift
    fit
    stay young
    workout
    what does it take
        eating healthy
        drop 10
        sleeker and sexier
        eating secrets
            makeup
            lose 10, 15, 20 pounds
            sizzling hot
            lost 10 pounds!
            relationship with food?
                    get-slim
                    not hungry.
                    a body to envy.
                    i don't have to eat anything
            best
        covergirl
    america's next top model
die
                            love,
                            beauty

i fucked up my teens

i wasted the short time i had. i thought i needed to be perfect; do exactly what others wanted, be who they envisioned—maybe then they would love me. i constantly chased impossible standards that made me forget I was alive.

i combined my last two years of high school. i studied all the time. i cried if i didn't get an A on a test. i had a 4.9 GPA and graduated with honors. i tried to force myself to exist. and all i got in return was the ability to bullshit an essay in under 20 minutes, crippling anxiety, and self-hatred so deeply ingrained that i didn't let myself eat.

i wish i had late night drives with my friends, blasting music, feeling free—like i was infinite and life could be euphoric. i wanted house parties and picnics with my partner. but I had days alone in my room, studying AP biology, taking practice ACT tests, planning how i could kill myself without hurting my family. i wanted road trips, hiking, discovering who i was and what life had to offer. but i let other people tell me what life would give me and how i would live.

i didn't make mistakes. i was perfect. so perfect i robbed myself of figuring out who i am.

daydream

lives made
for sugar plum dreams
they are not for me
see—
      i shouldn't still be here

to all the boys who pulled a gun on me

i love you.
i love the way you cared about me—
so passionate was your finger on the trigger.
so calming was your voice on the phone,
telling me how i caused your pain
i feel so at peace,
knowing that i can never trust anyone,
that the people i would die for
would rather have me dead.
so grateful i am to you
for giving me an experience we all go through
...right?
so reassuring it is to think
that you are always hovering outside the door.

to all the boys who pulled a gun on me,
i sincerely still love you.

song lyrics

oh they think about you
i think about you
i am the clouds
floating in the breeze

drive on the interstate
i live in outer space
get me out of the other lane

cold air from the freezer door
hair on my arm
flies away
bird lands in the tree

euphoria
cannot see
where am i?

i am in high school again

everything went back. i am a time traveler, living 16 again. i am back in control. i am the driver and i say my stomach is full. why is it always in threes? pinterest searches "lose weight fast". google asks "how much does a uterus way" as if i am going to cut out my own fucking uterus with a spoon to lose .16 pounds. well… no. no

daily routine

the first thing i do when i wake up is weigh myself. five pounds down from yesterday, i plan to lose three more today. i scroll through the dieting tips on my "random things" Pinterest board as the Keurig heats up water for my apple cider vinegar and lemon tea. i chug a couple glasses of water and fill up my water bottle. my dad is watching, so i grab a granola bar to throw in my lunchbox that already contains last week's moldy sandwich. at school, it feels like AP Bio is drowning on for hours. my mind is a war zone: fighting overeating low-cal popcorn and not eating at all. my mind urges me to pay attention to the teacher so i can ace the test tomorrow. finally, the bell rings.

at home, i drink another glass of water and change into workout clothes. i yell up at my mother, explaining that i'm going on a run to relieve some stress; she thinks it is a great idea. i don't know where i am in the neighborhood or how long i've been running but Bohemian Rhapsody snaps me back into reality and i notice my vision has gone black.

walking back to the house, slouched over in pain, i hold back my tears. i'm convinced that this is normal and healthy and it's best to keep one's over dramatic emotions to themselves. the Splenda from the zero-calorie sparkling ice drink revives me so that i can start my workout. Pinterest suggests toned legs and flat tummy. i pause every third sit up to take a sip of my drink so that my vision comes back. when i see my mom come downstairs to start dinner, i sneak off to the shower. 50 squats before i get into the cold water. my dad comes up to ask if i will join them for dinner. "sorry i just got out of the shower and i have a lot of homework to do". well, it wasn't a lie. i study for my six AP classes at the dining room table until my dad passes me on his way to bed. he says that i need to get some sleep; it's nearly midnight. so i go up to my room and wait for him to fall asleep before i go back down to study. eventually, i fall asleep, exhausted from a panic attack. i cry thinking about how i have to do it all again in 4 hours.

bakery

it's pretty hilarious
that i love to bake
an anorexic
who bakes

the universe is a
real fucking comedian

maybe it is an obsession
i can't eat it
if it is in
the oven
the smells will fill
my stomach

soft sky blue

quiet whisper wind
pure white clouds
perfection,
warmth,
endless vast beauty
consistency with you
my soft sky blue

thief

i could focus on the surface and say that it has caused me to miss out on life. i couldn't have dinner with my family, grab ice cream with my friends, or even have a conversation about where i wanted to eat. i could go a little further and tell you about how it has caused me not to be able to focus. all i could think about was food. it took my self-confidence and motivation to do anything. but if i'm being fully honest, i don't even know what it has taken. i just know that these are the right answers, that is what you want to hear, it's what is supposed to make me want to fight it. but i don't remember a time without it, so i can't say what i missed out on. who knows if my life would have been any different? all i can think about is what it has given me: an identity. something to focus on. a distraction. something i could be good at. a way out. a second plan. a way to finally feel something.

redemption

i must be more.
i must be better.
do you think
they will want me?

redeem me
                        my savior?

i deserve
nothing
i need
nothing
i am so far less than
nothing.

i am not here
i am not living
because i am not
                        real.

shower thoughts

4 a.m. getaway
you could be here with me
escape to neverland
discover my world
keep your eyes in the clouds
or you will hate me,
too

i scream
internally, silently
i can't wake the innocent—
ignorant
bash my head against the wall
smash my useless brain.
nails dig in my back
not too loud.

close my eyes
under the water
waves roll over
sinking,
drowning
and i am finally
breathing

my skin

my skin is fleshy pink
bright white
blends with the winter snow.

my skin takes my anger
and hides it.

bruises and scars,
my deepest secrets
safe beneath the surface
so no one will ever know.

ignorance

i think i am in love with you.

but then again,
whoever taught me how to love?

i am

disposable.

caffiene addiction

why does anxiety trump exhaustion? laying in the pitch black, realizing just how alone she is and she hates herself. she hates her body and her brain and resolves that she deserves to starve. to die— to vanish. she isn't worth food or love. she will never be worth anything.

caffeine trumps anxiety. it is better to numb the pain than to come to terms with emotions she can't ignore.

greetings

the kitchen's hello is the leftover smell
fried meat and roasted potatoes make me gag.
half-hearted peace signs and sporadic dancing
replace panicked crying and shaking on the floor.
is this my teens
or are we all just fucking depressed?

prom queen

blue eye
blondie
perfect body

soft waves
new clothes
slim waist

distant gaze
flowers and lace
simple hate.

cutting blades
sunken face
gain weight...

old wishes

i want to stare into your eyes, fixated in mine, while you babble out random facts and i nod along as though it is the most interesting information. i want to watch your hands gripping the paintbrush, smooth strokes on the canvas, wishing those hands were on my thighs. i would laugh when you smiled mid-kiss then you would go back to the candid sketch of me. i would daydream about days alone with you, going on picnics and getting drunk in your studio. we would watch ghost documentaries and dance with the rain blasting One Direction until we were so tired, we collapse on the couch, with my head on your chest captured in a polaroid picture.

greetings (pt. 2)

courage comes to lurk from my safe space
instead of "hello, how are you?"
i am met with the details of my mother's new diet
and calorie counts of the muffins I baked
my only source of sustainment last week
i slice my apple,
retreat back to my hideout
instead of sweet honey crisp
i taste burning stomach acid.
rotting on my desk for three days
is reminder:
i am in control.

beginnings

it started because I wanted to be happy. i needed them to want me. i thought external forces could convince me i was alive. eventually, i figured out the universe is a liar and i was pissed. but i have only ever felt anger toward myself. so i took out frustration on my skin—on my body. finally, that became all i could feel. numbness was more pain than dying. so I chose death.

escape: my only friend

what am i?

my brain isn't attached to my body because i am not real. my body is manufactured, and my thoughts are all i have and my thoughts are home, and they are safe, and they are yelling at me to feel. to feel anything— something. but I don't know how to feel because my body has been broken down, disassembled into all its parts. my limbs have all gone numb, so they scream, "stop!" stop feeling. stop being. stop existing. you are not real if you aren't really feeling. numbness is death, so why is my body still hanging on when my mind is calling it to join the thoughts in my grave?

mantra

food is not your friend.
calories won't make you happy.
food is not your friend.
calories won't make you happy.
food is not your friend.
calories won't make you happy.
food is not your friend.
calories won't make you happy.
food is not your friend.
calories won't make you happy.
food is not your friend.
calories won't make you happy.
food is not your friend.
calories won't make you happy.
food is not your friend.
calories won't make you happy.
food is not your friend.
calories won't make you happy.
food is not your friend.
calories won't make you happy.
food is not your friend.
calories won't make you happy.
food is not your friend.
calories won't make you happy.
food is not your friend.
calories won't make you happy.
calories won't make you happy.
calories won't make you happy.
calories won't make you happy.
calories won't make you happy.
food is not your friend.

ww3

my brain is world war three and i don't have a helmet. i have no fucking clue what i am supposed to do. it should be simple, or at least possible. they should be able to tell me it is hurting and there is a cure and that should be enough. but, to me, enough is a fantasy—a made-up word in Dr. Seuss books. nothing will ever be enough. i can never be enough until i wither away to dust—until i don't exist. i don't need to be told how to get healthy. what i need is to want to exist. to feel like i am real and all this shit is worth it. all i have is empty promises but only she can hear it.

privacy

it has always been a private thing: no one was ever supposed to hear my cry for help or notice my bleeding heart. i starved myself for me, i burned my skin for me to feel—i was never meant to be seen. i do not want to burden; i am my own obligation. please, do not pay attention. i want to be small—unnoticed. blend in until I can no longer be pointed out.

i fade away.

and no.

i don't want you to fix me.
let me destroy myself
from the inside out.
let me mutilate my body
and burn off my skin.
let me watch
myself fade away
because all i truly want
is to become a part of the shadows.

her?

was i supposed to know
who i am
who do they want
her?

skinny
basic
bitch
you're just copying
fake
who are you
her?

authentic self
natural
ugly
fat
lose some fucking weight
who is she
her?

not her.
they do not want her.
they could never love
her.

breathe

my body is at the table. my hand is reaching for the glass of water. drinking. i am there but my head is drowning. the waves crashing above me, the current carries me to the seabed and i am asleep. and no one offers a life raft. i don't want one. i am okay. i belong here. i was meant to drown—

sink—

sleep

beauty in darkness

she is a dark mystery novel, begging you not to turn the page. an edgy storm's chaos blinding the world from the truth. but her laugh knows how to live and her smile knows how to feel for others. and, one day, it will feel for itself, too.

real

you are real.
you are beautiful.
you are seen.
you are enough.
you are worth it.
you are alive.

we will figure out
a way to feel
if we figure out
that we are real.

i want you to exist.

daydream (pt. 2)

dancing in the rain,
soft music pouring down
spinning, smiling, laughing
serotonin yelling
"you are alive"
you exist in the perfect moment
life is enough.

you eat for me

and i'll eat for you.

i don't want...

to see you go.

true beauty

she is the beauty in the chaos of living

scrambled eggs

thoughts are loud
buzzing noises in our brains
scrambling together.
i don't have a voice

they tell me
i will only find silence in death
but silence is numb,
deafening.

noise is laughter,
love,
people.
noise is life.

and life will be okay
eventually.
push out the buzzing
until we can hear

most

why do the people
who mean the most
only get to see the start
and never the end result?

for her

i never understood the word home. it felt foreign—a fantasy land in storybooks only meant for princesses to experience. home is where you belong, like it was destiny for you to be placed in that exact spot. i was never given a spot. a nomad wandering from house to house looking for somewhere to want me. home didn't exist until nothing existed. and there she was...

my home. inside a beautiful girl with straight pink hair who couldn't see that she was the perfect place. home wore crop tops and leggings and made self-deprecating jokes. but home showed me how to exist with myself. home showed me i belong here. home filled my missing bricks.

she is my home

mine

if you are my person
i will give you my world
excavating my own land

because when i love you
you are so much more
than i could ever be mourned

querencia

sunshine-filled water droplets
    roll off the tip of her nose
pull me in close
    wash away the pain
my querencia
    and i
are one home

existing obsolete

sitting on the ground, soaking in the water droplets, wishing i was Harry Styles's music video, drowning myself and my piano. but my words are not that deep and i can never reach starving artist. i am here and they have taken that. i am separate from my rain. separate from my self. existing alone, dreaming up suicide pacts that mean more than love letters. hold hands and we can jump together. making bracelets that mean nothing just to numb the feeling of everything.

existing

obsolete.

idk

i don't know how to convince her because i can't even prove it to myself. i could never reach it because i am not worth it. but she is. so i can pretend for myself if i can show her it is okay to live. the living have a future and she does too.

give up

i just want it to be over. the voices are so fucking loud and mine isn't even in the mix anymore. yelling so loud i cannot hear. i must drown the voices, it's the only way to find silence—peace. it will be over. it will be quiet. i can breathe.

let me be

selfish.

fake

i ate. it should be as simple as that: i ate. but i failed. i should make up for it because all i am is lying to the world. i so desperately want to tell the truth so i try to let it out but it lies in a pit. A well at the bottom of my stomach that has been collecting bad thoughts, bad feelings—bad. i wish i could drain out the lies but i am fake. as fake as a pretty pink pen writing depressing-as-hell words, pretending that they are bubble gum. i sit in the library and stare at my book; i smile, i laugh. but it is not real because real is only for the living. the future is only for those that are alive, i have been dead so long my breathing body only carries on the lie. she is fake. she is not there. she is not real.

clinomania

noun.
the excessive desire to stay in bed
the desire to eat everything in the pantry
or to eat nothing at all
the feeling of dread
and internal chaos
intrusive thoughts saying
you can't lift your arms.
yelling at you to just die already
the inability to ask for help
or call your friend.
the pain of 12 lifetimes
wishing you didn't have to
carry it all.

clinomania:
noun.
depression.

paintings

we are paintbrushes, coloring the canvas vibrant yellows. the hills and the grass—a small stream of rushing turquoise. i want a rainbow; sun rays after the storm. cloudless skies of blue, all just for you.

but you said you could not paint with me. your canvas was filled with color. my paintbrush was worn thin; the bristles collecting on the canvas. i left splinters in your fingers. so you picked up a new and i snapped myself in two.

past/future

the past is the past and we're past it. but the past is my home. and it has inflicted so much damage on the future now all it is is a lone house—beaten and berated—stealing bricks and pieces from my heart so that is so much different from the start. but my home has scraps of patterned fabric, stored to patch up my holes. yet, i will never be whole if i am always so alone.

scrambling eggs

whisking scrambled eggs
blackened in my brain
they yell,
"i will never go away"
they scream to be let out
i don't know the way out
they want out
they want out!
someone let them out!
i can't get them out!
they are burning up my brain
steaming without a fire extinguisher
show me the emergency exit
let them out!

sad

sad is teardrops
welling up, under my eyes—
let the floodgates flow

sad is utter exhaustion
my heart drops to the floor
unable to be lifted

sad is the well
at the bottom of my stomach;
it won't fill

sad is my eyes
burning when I try to sleep
will they ever close?

sad is my legs won't move,
pick up my arms
please let me out of bed!

sad is racing thoughts,
galloping horses in my brain
stop winning the race

sad is
i can't do this anymore.
please...

laughing

and i am there…

who, what, when, where, why?

crying in the back seat of the car
where am i
they do not want me
no one wants me
i can't do this anymore
i can't keep lying
but the truth is too painful
i am a liar
if only i could tell him

desire

hovering above
      my personal storm cloud
   i want to be
          a rainbow

life fucking sucks

it sucks when you get caught in a storm. it sucks when you drop your phone on your face. it sucks when you catch a cold. it sucks when you can't remember the last time you laughed. it sucks when you no longer know how to be happy. it sucks when you don't want to be here anymore. life fucking sucks.

but i hope it will get better...

one day

i can hear the music
one day
i can stand in an isle
and i am there
one day
we can drive as far as we want
and i won't disappear
one day
we will be real
one day.

we are enough

i want to be happy.

still

they will still be there;
and i will be, too

concede

i try to convince myself i deserve it but i am so selfish for still wanting it. it is not for me. i can never deserve anything. give it to them.

how?

i know i want to be happy and i want to live a life that is worth it but why does my mind say the only way to live is if i am small, if no one can see me. the only way i can exist is if no one can tell because all i am is an inconvenience. how do i live happily if i cannot exist?

rock bottom

rock bottom
does not exist
i am
rock bottom

daydream (pt. 3)

sugarplum dreams of two kids, suburban homes, PTA bake sales, and soccer games fade into wishes of running away to a hidden cottage near a pond in the woods. one small bedroom, antique cat figurines. living room with a tiny flower-patterned couch, cat resting. butterfly kisses wish me awake in the morning. we sip our coffee outside, listening to the birds sing. i water my plants, work in the garden, bake cookies, write whatever i want—happy poems. wind rustles leaves, turns the pages of our book. she kisses me goodnight, warm side-by-side until the sun's aubade invites us to another euphoric life.

what's different this time?

i am trying to validate
myself.

missing you

the day will come
when you can't cover up
what you've done

they will see the scars
they will notice the untouched plate
they will read the letters

and you will see their eyes
hear them crying
late at night
scared to lose you

so don't lose your fight,
kid
or we'll be missing you.

my inspiration

she is a sun i look directly up at. it burns my eyes but all i want is to be that. the sun is beautiful and kind, it brings new life with its light. she sparks fires of hope, dreams i have only dreamt of having.

one day, i will hold the earth in my hand, and i will open that door to see the passion the sun sees in the world

growth

a bambi shaped ceramic pot
the leaves are growing so i thought
flowers bloom before they rot
maybe we have wilted

wind whisperer

the wind whispers, softly in my ear,
"fly away with me. you can be free"
but i am pulled down by the rain
"stay with me"

wishes

i wish i had paid more attention
when i started getting sick
i lied and lied
"i'm fine" was my truth
if i knew myself
i would have noticed

yet, maybe that is the problem
i know my inner thoughts,
my deepest secrets
and i hate her.

and so would you.

i'm fine

the most ignorant questions are those that can only be answered with a lie.

loser

"when was the last time you got lost"

i have always been lost. the question you should be asking is, *when will i be found?*

existence

i can't exist with myself
until my self comes into existence

there is no one answer

you ask me "why?" and i stare blankly into your eyes. there is no acceptable response to give. no singular person or thing fucked me up. so, if you ask me "why?" i will respond with "i".

open my fridge

if you opened my fridge you would find rotten grapes and expired cream cheese. a bottle of unopened ketchup and a full ice machine. you would find secrets and fears stashed away behind chunky milk. you would find isolation and despair. but, one day, you will open my fridge and find hope.

recovery

i am recovering from hating myself.

from years of yelling into the mirror, you are not enough. months of writing you are not worth food, over and over again. days of cursing out my body and my brain, wishing they would just go away.

i am recovering from myself

i would buy happiness

hand it out on the streets like balloons full of smiles. give it to kids that just learned they have a body and should be ashamed of it. to women who have been robbed of their safety. to men who think they are not allowed to cry. to people who don't remember when they last laughed.

i would buy happiness and give it to the world.

dear kids

who just realized they have a body,

your body does not determine your future
your body does not determine your worth
your body does not determine who you can be
your body does not determine success
your body does not define you.

stop sign

yells at me "halt"
patiently wait,
the time will come
when it is safe
to go again.

when i was a kid,

the world was sunshine and rainbows
until someone told me
it shouldn't be
now i can't remember
when i last smelled the roses

canvas

they sit down at the table and stare at the words on my canvas—never truly reading me. i wish they could hear me. i would tell them they deserve this and only speak the truth. i could gain their trust and they could finally say to their body, softly, "i want to be your friend". i would take a deep breath and whisper back, "i have been waiting my whole life for this."

beautiful music

the sound of my stomach growling is music to my ears, lyrics i haven't heard in years; the pain is familiar and comforting—like reconnecting with a best friend. but she no longer speaks to me; i told her she was the boy who cried wolf until the wolf came, and i didn't. now i sing along without the music

reasons to not die:

your best friend
your pets
your family
the first sip of coffee in the morning
new experiences
first kisses
crushes that give you butterflies
there are new people to meet
new music to hear
art you haven't seen
places you haven't been
restaurants you haven't tried
experiences you haven't had
details you haven't learned about yourself
cars you haven't driven in
parties you haven't gone to
cats you haven't adopted
people you have yet to love
a life you have yet to live
because you have nothing left to lose

reasons to live:

...

i could never

i would never hurt you
but i kill everyone around me
i must run from my existence
because all i cause is pain

i could never hurt you
so i must get away

i flee

when i am a burden
when i am an inconvenience
when i hurt people
when i make someone mad
when i do something wrong
when i don't think they want me
when i am afraid,
i flee.

i knew when…

we were in your studio, you were painting, i was fully entranced; i couldn't look away. all I wanted were your hands to paint me.

we were at the radio station late at night watching one direction videos. we kept spinning in our chairs, timing it so our legs kept bumping.

we were at the coffee shop and you bought my coffee because i was too anxious to order. you sat down next to me, our thighs were side by side, sharing our heat.

we were on campus, drunk. i was jumping on a trampoline and i sat down—imagining what it could be like to sit in your lap.

we were in your bed, knees touching, watching captain america, drunk off our asses. i wanted to lean over and kiss you—blame it on the alcohol.

we were walking around campus and were so tired we collapsed in the grass and looked up at the stars. i just wanted to grab your hand.

we were in your dorm, i jokingly put on your hat, you tied a scarf around my neck, lightly holding my waist while looking in the mirror. "it looks better on you."

i looked into your eyes and knew

i knew nothing.

always

i'll always be the quiet, shy girl you thought was a bitch when you first met her.

plead

someone needs to design a better world
a world where gender and sexuality doesn't matter
where climate change isn't up for debate
where kids can be kids,
where people feel safe,
where there is laughter,
where diet magazines and thinspo don't exist,
where models are normal people,
where we care about personalities and not bodies,
a world where people can just exist.

magic eraser

i want to erase the kids who told me I was fat. i want to erase the overheard conversations of my parents being worried about my weight. i want to erase the boys laughing after they asked me out as a joke. i want to erase looking into the mirror at dance class, realizing how much bigger i was than the other girls. i want to erase dressing room mirrors that screamed you are too fat for that outfit. i want to erase thinspo on Pinterest. i want to erase boiled egg diets and intermittent fasting. i want to erase 30-day ab challenges and flat-tummy toners. i want to erase meal replacement shakes and 100 calorie snacks. i want to erase being afraid of soda. of candy. of food. of life.

i want to erase my need to be enough for someone.

raindrop

drip...drip...drip
ever dribbling
streaming from the clouds

many see only misery
seeping into their socks
everlasting dampness on their clothes
sorrow,
dread,
despair.
pushing it away,
blocking her from soaking their hair

but she is my home
bringing me peace,
safety,
security,
hope,
tranquility.
i let her swallow me,
drowning my thoughts,
carrying me away
engrossed in her glory

oh,
how i long for the rain
for her to come,
and drift me away

starving

i starve myself. even when i'm hungry. even when i craved those fries. even when my parents get worried. even when i meet my "goal" weight. even when i feel like shit. even when i pass out running in the neighborhood. even when i want nothing more than to just be able to eat, i starve myself.

search history

how many calories are in an apple?
is cashew milk healthier than almond?
what is my bmi?
how much should i weigh?
lowest calorie meal at applebees.
how to throw up.
quick workouts.
how many calories does running burn?
zero calorie foods.
30-day diet challenge.
how can i kill myself?

it exists

laughter exists
rain exists
dancing exists
singing exists
joy
happiness
euphoria
life
i exist.

this is it

this is the moment
i am finally alive
and i want to be
live in those little moments
please,
for me,
for the rain

dear future sad me,

you are real. life isn't fake—you saw its reality. dancing in the rain and you are free and you are happy and you are there. and you are alive. don't leave because the rain is worth staying for; you are worth staying for.

give zero fucks

in the right direction

she is

the one who told me to stay
the one who said she felt the same way
the one who danced in the rain
the one who held my hand while we laid
the one who said she didn't want me to go away
the one who explained she can relate
the one who never missed a day
the one who said crying is okay
the one who asked me to live
she is my hope.

they raised me

the boy who played house when we were 4
the girls across the street who played with me
the brother and sister who called us family
the girl who pretended we were mermaids
the neighborhood kids who let us jump on their trampoline
the girl who shared my goldfish
the girl who did crafts with me
the person whose nose i accidentally broke
the girls that i fought with constantly
the people i met my first day
who became friends for life
the people i knew less than a week
that changed my life forever

fake

fake it till you make it; keep going through the motions and one day it will be true and you will be real. we can feel, i promise.

transparency

laying upside down, toes pointed to the sky, her hand is in mine. softly singing "you can't cover up what you've done". and she heard me. in that moment i was real and our pain was real and she was willing to see me. i thought my scars were so blinding but i've just been surrounded by those who told me to hide.

she saw me

favorite place?

my favorite place is the coffee shop where you said you had feelings for me. you bought my coffee and sat down beside me, our knees bumped together, so i shifted, pressing my leg up against yours. they were talking but all i heard was your body's heat and your eyes fixated in mine. i wonder what i did to make you stop.

favorite place.

my favorite place is right here. sitting on the squishy chair and i sink into it. she sits beside me. and someone finally understands. two butterflies come out of their cocoons to fly away like they were meant to. my favorite place is home.

meeting myself

she tiptoed into the room without saying a thing. she silently sat down in the chair beside me. i could see the pain in her eyes. i could see myself in her eyes.

"it's going to be okay"

she grew more comfortable with each passing day, opening up to me. she told me why she was here and who had hurt her and i could finally say "me too".

she read me her words. i couldn't tell which lines were hers and which were from my own mouth but it didn't matter because we weren't real anyways.

"i want you to stay"

energetic is

energetic is
    happy
    energetic is
    joyful
energetic is
    excitement
energetic is
    jumping up and down
energetic is
    blood rushing to my head
energetic is
    running around the house
energetic is
    screaming along to the music
energetic is
    taking for myself
energetic is
    selfish
energetic is

hopeful

hope is the scariest emotion.

i hope i will get better
but fret over getting worse.
i hope i will want it
but i am worried i will give up.
i hope he will love me
but i am frightened of being alone.
i hope i will always hope
but i am scared of losing.

i hope one day
hope won't hurt so much.

girls

her eyes
no…
her mouth
her hands
her smile
her body
her everything

girls are so fucking beautiful.

she

i turn up the volume
singing the way
she smells sweet
i exhale slowly
softly as her skin
legs gravitate
finding each other
pulling her in

whispers
she
means everything
to me.

butterflies

flying high
with the clouds
looking for
a place
that's safe
destiny
will find them
and bring
the two
home

i love you is

have you eaten yet
i love you is
call me when you get home
i love you is
pulling the blanket over cold legs
i love you is
hold your hand when you are nervous
i love you is
a soft kiss on the cheek
i love you is
i feel your pain
i understand you
you are not alone

i love you is
i want you here

hostage

everything is the unknown. and the unknown is terrifying because it holds failure and failure is death and death is hope and hope is life and life is success and success is future and the future is unknown and the unknown holds failure hostage. unknown holds me hostage.

i am not a hostage

together

she is the unknown
and the unknown holds excitement
and excitement holds fear
and fear holds us in the palm of its hand
and that hand holds us together

desperation

he calls me
desperate to talk
and so lonely
i am frightened
made speechless from his tone
secret threats
fake apologies
"you bitch"
"you broke him"
i am deceitful
        crude
                destructive
                        broken

they want to die
i should die
they can be happy—
he can be happy

dear 13-year-old,

you are not that powerful. you are not the grim reaper in human flesh, here to choose who dies. you do not maintain that balance. you cannot control him.

so be selfish. have something to give. you have my permission to exist.

sincerely,

the rain

future promises

she is sitting in the sand, watching the sunrise over the ocean, sipping iced coffee. a girl sits beside her and hands her breakfast. she stares into her eyes, watching the waves roll softly to shore. she tries to write but the girl surfing in the distance makes it impossible to write about anything else.

they bake bread in the little cafe, talking and laughing with the regulars. after the store clears, they hand the extra loaves to those in need.

they go on a drive with the roof down. it starts to sprinkle so they pull over and dance in the rain.

they return home to take a hot shower. pulling on warm sweaters and cuddling by the fireplace. she reads her new poetry.

she doesn't have everything figured out. maybe she isn't doing what she planned to. she's not with who she thought she would be. she lives somewhere different. she doesn't make everyone happy, but that's okay because she is happy. she has people that love her, and she lets them. she is content. she wants to be alive—and, for once, she is.

i would live for myself

i will live for myself

praise for
we're not real anyways

Maddie Mitchell's book is a clarion call from the war zone of anorectic suffering. Her poems unveil and call to account the forces and indignities that imperil young women by pressuring them to be perfect and small. This is an emotionally searing, impressively crafted sequence that intertwines its statement of truth with an ongoing search for hope. It is the work of a talented young poet whose voice is haunting, inspiring and indelible.

—Barbara Burch, PhD,
Professor of English, Georgetown College

Right from the title, Maddie Mitchell plays with the reader's doubts of reality and invites us into her mindset and into her personal experiences that are easily translated to the universal by happenings that have let her down, that let us down as we yearn throughout life for approval and acceptance. Within these intensely feminine and young experiences there is also such love amid Mitchell's words. With the intense title of "to all the boys who pulled a gun on me," and with those initial words of that piece, *i love you*, it shows that Mitchell understands it is not just her that yearns for this love.

These poems hold such an innocent intelligence and would be an incredible gift to read for young people, people struggling, and especially for those that don't seem to be struggling as well. If young people were encouraged to read such common and powerful feelings, it might make a positive difference within themselves. What these poems reveal is how we should shed more light and place more emphasis on young mental health and stop condemning people from certain thoughts and emotions. We should be listening and opening our arms in acceptance. In the poem "ww3," she labels the feeling of *enough* as only found in Dr. Seuss books. There is not an in-between anymore; it's either good or not good enough. The unfiltered abandon that Mitchell is able to confess in each poem for us is admirable.

—Rebecca Smolen, author of *Excoriation*,
Gateless Method facilitator

about the author

maddie mitchell is an 18-year-old poet and writer from paris, kentucky. she graduated from bourbon county high school in 2019, one year earlier than expected, and began attending georgetown college at age 17. she is currently a sophomore and plans to major in english and political science with a minor in spanish. she hopes to one day attend law school in order to become an immigration lawyer. she is also a part of the oxford honors program at her college and plans to spend a semester or two at oxford university in england in the coming years.

the young writer deferred a semester of college during her sophomore year to focus on treatment for several mental illnesses including borderline personality disorder, anxiety, major depressive disorder, obsessive-compulsive disorder, and anorexia nervosa. she was at a residential treatment facility for her eating disorder for over 11 weeks, and she then went through several step-down stages of the recovery process over the span of several months. throughout this process, she wrote many of the poems included in *we're not real anyways*. her book also speaks on topics of feminism and lgbtq+ romances. she has hopes that her poetry is relatable to others who deal with similar issues discussed in this, her first book, *we're not real anyways*.

pronouns: she/they
instagram: @maddie.h.m
facebook: maddie.mitchell.969
tiktok: @maddie.h.m

About The Poetry Box®

The Poetry Box® is a boutique publishing company in Portland, Oregon, which provides a platform for both established and emerging poets to share their words with the world through beautiful printed books and chapbooks.

Feel free to visit the online bookstore (thePoetryBox.com), where you'll find more titles including:

Excoriation by Rebecca Smolen

Motherhood & Other Scars by Rebecca Smolen

Staring Down the Tracks in Hope by Julia Paul

Just the Girls by Pamela Anderson

Before the Distance by Pasquale Trozzolo

World Gone Zoom by David Belmont

The Screaming Silence by Lanser Howard

Hello, Darling by Christine Higgins

Shoebox by Donovan Hufnagle

Building a Woman by Deborah Meltvedt

(good cape weather) by Traj Wes

What She Was Wearing by Shawn Aveningo Sanders

Protection by Michelle Lerner

and more . . .

www.ingramcontent.com/pod-product-compliance
Lightning Source LLC
LaVergne TN
LVHW012112070526
838202LV00056B/5703